I AM

A 7-Day Devotional of Prayer and Healing

REGINA ATKINSON

Copyright © 2021 Regina Atkinson

ALL RIGHTS RESERVED. This book contains material protected under International and Federal Copyright Laws and Treaties. Any unauthorized reprint or use of this material is prohibited. No part of this book may be reproduced or transmitted in any form or by any means, electronic or mechanical, including photocopying, recording, or by any information storage and retrieval system without express written permission from the author/publisher.

Unless otherwise noted all Scripture, quotations are taken from the King James Version of the Bible. All rights reserved.

Scripture is taken from the New King James Version®. Copyright © 1982 by Thomas Nelson. All rights reserved.

Book Cover Design: Prize Publishing House

Printed by: Prize Publishing House, LLC in the United States of America.

First printing edition 2021.
Prize Publishing House
P.O. Box 9856, Chesapeake, VA 23321
www.PrizePublishingHouse.com

ISBN (Paperback): 978-1-7374791-8-5
ISBN (E-Book): 978-1-7374791-9-2

Contents

Foreword 4

Day 1: Daddy's Girl (You Are God's Girl) 6

Day 2: I Am Not What The World Says I Am...11

Day 3: God Check My Heart................................16

Day 4: Decree It, Declare It! 22

Day 5: Surrounded By Love (God Surround Us With Love)..27

Day 6: Heal My Broken Spirit..............................32

Day 7: I'm Moving On 38

Foreword

When one thinks of beauty, the first thought that may come to mind is something pleasant to behold or pleasing to the eye. Beauty can be external, but some of the most beautiful things are not physically seen. Inner beauty is cultivated through one's experiences and self-realization. It is developed through the mind, body, and soul.

Do not allow the things of the world and the perception of others to define who you are, but be confident in knowing who you are in God.

Join Regina on this 7-day journey to discovering who you are in the Lord. When you have a relationship with the Father and know that you are made in His image, you are unstoppable!!

You are confident to walk in who He has made you to be and can conquer anything.

The world has its own set of standards and expectations, but who do you say you are? Most importantly, who does God say you are?

As you take this journey, affirm to yourself that you are beautiful. You are fearfully and wonderfully made. We all go through things, but what we do with those experiences cultivates our true beauty and who we are. Love who you are on your journey to healing from the inside out, for it is through the process that God creates His most amazing masterpieces!!

Pastor Shavon Smith

Day 1

Daddy's Girl (You Are God's Girl)

Growing up, I have always been a daddy's girl. I know what true love really means because of the love my daddy gave and still gives to me. I mean, I used to get on mommy's nerves because I was such a spoiled brat. I got my way ALL the time. Daddy always reminded me from a little girl that I was beautiful.

He reminded me that I was beautiful with my natural hair, my natural nails, and without makeup. Even when I gained weight and felt fat, my father would always encourage me. He would tell me that if I did not like the weight, I could work out and do it for myself not just to "look good" but also to be healthy. He always let me know I was created in the image of God and that there was nothing wrong with me. Wow, I would like to say that I am a blessed woman to have the love and presence of my daddy even in this present time. Having a caring dad, as I have, has set the tone for what love should be…..unconditional.

I believe that it's crucial to a young girl growing up to have a father in her life and a present one at that. It shapes and molds her. It shapes her because it helps how she views men. Having a great example in a father helps guide that. It molds her because she will be able to know what unconditional love is. If she experiences something contrary, she will know that her worth is far above accepting anything less because her father always set the tone.

As I would venture into my teen and adult years, I didn't realize that I would experience questioning a lot of what I did know, but I would always be brought back to reality with reminders of daddy's love. I never wanted to disappoint daddy or mommy. Being that I am an only girl, the pressure was on me. Growing up in the church, the pressure was on me. I wouldn't say I was sheltered because I wasn't. My parents were excellent parents who raised us right and loved us so much. When I say us, I'm talking about my three brothers and me. We grew up in Queens, New York, so we were a little rough around the edges but still had all the tools instilled in us to be somebody great in this world.

Takeaway

Remember all I said as it relates to my father's love because this will be brought up again later and will be an essential piece of this story. My prayer for you is that you will always know that you are loved no matter what walk of life you may find yourself in. From the girl who had their dad around from a little girl to the girl who didn't know who her dad was, know that you are loved so much by the Father. God loves you with an everlasting love that cannot be broken. Jeremiah 31:3 states, "Yea, I have loved thee with an everlasting love: therefore with lovingkindness have I drawn thee." Everlasting means lasting forever. That's some kind of love!! God loves you with an everlasting love and despite how it started for you, know that God is here now and will always be. You are God's Girl. You are his beloved. What are some things you want to tell God about where you are? What do you want Him to help you with?

Prayer

Father God, in the name of Jesus, help my sister understand who you really are and that you love her unconditionally. Wherever she feels she lacks love, make up for it in every area of her life. Lord, fill every void. I ask that that you will lift her this day from any feelings of abandonment! In Jesus' name. Amen.

Day 2

I Am Not What The World Says I Am

Now that you know where I come from, I want to tell you that just because I have a loving father who still tells me these wonderful things doesn't mean I didn't encounter challenges that made me question the things I knew. At the age of 16, I was a teenage mother and in my senior year of high school. I found myself in a dark place. I was scared and worried because I didn't want to disappoint my mom and dad. Mommy was disappointed, but from a mother to a daughter, she had a sensitive spot for me at that moment. Daddy was the opposite. He was upset. He was angry because he did not want that for me at that time. But, the love for me never wavered. He waited a few days, and then he went ahead and mended things with me. Again, reminding me that he loved me and was there for my unborn child and me.

Sometimes I heard the kids' whispers in school saying things like, "She's a loser," "She's pregnant," and shaking their heads at me. I didn't want to be a statistic. I didn't want to be what the world said that I was. When I found out I was pregnant, I thought about aborting him because I was scared and worried about what people would say. But when I began to feel the little flutters and kicks,

I Am Beautifully Me:
A 7-Day Devotional of Prayer and Healing

there was no way I could do that. I surely did not believe in abortion, but I was so worried about being labeled. I had to understand that we have that unconditional love in our heavenly Father, even in our mistakes. I repented. I asked Him to forgive me and kept my baby. That baby is now 14 years old.

That experience at such a young age truly caused me to grow. I was able to finish high school despite the odds. I actually brought my baby to my graduation. God showed me that even in my error, He was still with me. See, often in our lives, we make mistakes, and we do things we are not proud of, but what we have to do is learn from these mistakes. Allow God to heal and bring you to a place of repentance and move forward. We serve a forgiving God. We fall so much, but His grace and His mercy keep us. I always believed He forgives, but I don't have to keep making the same mistakes because, after that, it is just intentional. I am not what the world says that I am.

Takeaway

Understand that we all make mistakes, and the Bible says we all sin and fall short of the glory of God. This is not the moment to beat yourself up for what was already done, but to learn from it and show our heavenly Father that we repent and have the heart to live right. We all have to learn to forgive ourselves for where we have been, so we can move into the place where God is taking us. What are some things you have asked God to forgive you for? List some things you feel you need to forgive yourself for. Give it to God and let Him heal.

Prayer

Father God, in the name of Jesus, I pray that you help my dear sister to forgive. I pray that she forgives herself for the things that have been keeping her bound. Touch her heart, mind, and spirit that she would trust You even more. Help her know she is loved and that she has so much more in her that You may use her for Your glory. Something good is coming out of this. In Jesus' name. Amen.

Day 3

God Check My Heart

After having my baby, I struggled with my appearance because I carried baby weight from having a child. Society tells you you're beautiful *if*, you are wanted *if*. I was self-conscious. I began to assume the mentality that I wasn't beautiful if I didn't look a certain way. I was a 17-year-old single mother just out of high school.

I knew the scripture Psalm 139:14 that was always quoted in church, "I will praise thee; for I am fearfully and wonderfully made." I told you that I was a daddy's girl and I was certainly always reminded I was beautiful. But at a point, I wanted validation from others. I wanted my friends to say, "Girl, you did that." I wanted the boys to tell me, "You are absolutely beautiful." I sought after that. I waited for it. Not realizing that I did not need that at all. But this definitely started something in me that would then spiral out of control.

I desperately wanted to believe that I was made in His image as His word said. I wanted to believe that I was more than enough. I wanted to believe that I loved what I was looking at in the mirror. But I was up against the random thoughts that the enemy would make me think about myself. The reality is that the validation I wanted the father of my child to give me was not enough. That after everyone else told me how gorgeous I was, I was still left feeling a little empty. God was going to show me what He sees in me eventually.

Have you ever felt as though you weren't beautiful because after the social media influencers came on and everyone flocked to them, you started feeling like you wanted to change everything about yourself? I've seen so many people hurting because they felt inadequate. Maybe you felt a way because people around you had all the money and could buy designer clothes, but here you are wearing Walmart outfits. Let me tell you, let it not be that you are dressed in all these designer labels but have no heart for people. One thing I knew I didn't want to be was a pretty dressed-up mess. I knew that at least my heart was pure, and I loved people. Sometimes I asked God how did He end up making me this way? I asked this because people would hurt me, and I would love them like they never did anything or continued as the offense never happened. But He again let me know that I have HIS heart.

I was reminded when David was anointed King in 1 Samuel 16, Samuel was sent to Jesse's house to anoint the next King, and when he arrived, God would let him know who he was to anoint. So, upon seeing one of Jesse's sons first, he thought surely this has got to be him. But God had to have a little sidebar talk with Samuel that he figured this was the one by merely looking upon his outward appearance. He quickly let him know that man looks at the outward appearance, but God looks at the heart. While society tries to say what is considered "it," God reminds people to look at the heart. Check your heart and re-evaluate.

Takeaway

Do not get so carried away in the outward appearance of a thing because God is surely looking at the man's heart. You are fierce! You are bold! You are beautiful! He created you, and He did not make junk. Search your heart today and allow God to cleanse your heart and mind of thinking the way the world thinks. You may feel you don't have all the things other people have, but I can tell you that you have GOD. Let Him do the work in you so that He can renew your heart and mind. Transform your thinking.

Prayer

Father God, in the name of Jesus, search my dear sister's heart, reminding her that she should strive to fit Your mold, not the one the world created. Help her to be kind to people always and to have a heart more like Yours. God, I thank You for her life today that she is shifting even now getting into position. Just like David, God knew He could use him because of the condition of his heart; use her for Your glory. In Jesus' name. Amen.

Day 4

Decree It, Declare It!

When you have a relationship with God, He will often keep sending you subtle reminders of who you are. But, also understand that the enemy will try to contradict what God says concerning you. One thing I had to do was get into the word of God and really start applying the word to every area of my life. I started seeing myself in the word when I was low, and there was always a remedy there for my situation.

Now, when I say the enemy will literally try to contradict what the Lord says. I mean it because

I Am Beautifully Me:
A 7-Day Devotional of Prayer and Healing

that is what he tried to do to me many years after I had children and became an Evangelist. He still tested me. Whenever the Lord would say, "Regina, I called you," the enemy would say, "Did He really call you?" When God would send reminders that I was beautiful, the enemy would say, "Really? Do you believe that?" When God would say, "You will be the mother, wife, daughter, sister, friend, and Evangelist I called you to be," the enemy would try to put so much doubt in me that I wouldn't be able to meet the requirements to be those things God said I would be. I did have challenges, but when I would entertain the enemy's thoughts, I began to realize that I saw myself in a negative light when I knew that was contrary to what the Lord said that I was.

You have to stop giving the enemy access and an opportunity to speak negatively into your spirit concerning you at a point in your life. Why? Because you can combat it with the word of God. Why? Because the word of God is true, and the word of God brings life. So, whenever you start feeling low and feeling unworthy, remember who your daddy is and get back into the posture of prayer and decreeing and declaring over your life. I can tell you that you are an amazingly beautiful person inside and out. But to you, the person who may have insecure thoughts about yourself, you will still doubt it. You will look in the mirror and find a million and one things wrong with you.

I want to challenge you on this 4th day to start declaring and decreeing over your life that you will begin to see the manifestation of the word. The word of God teaches us many things about the way that God sees us. Again, we are fearfully and wonderfully made. We are the head and not the tail. We are above and not beneath. We are everything God says we are. You may not see it, but I challenge you to start saying it until you see it.

Takeaway

Today is the day you start decreeing and declaring over your life as you are sitting in expectation for God to do the miraculous in your life. You may feel like you don't see it, and it seems so hard to obtain. But the point of faith again is to believe what you don't see, knowing that God has your back and He won't let you fall. Look in the mirror today and start decreeing and declaring over yourself that what God says about you is true. Let Him know your struggle and that you need His help. That's what He is here for. The reality is He already knows what you need, and He already knows your struggle. Speak your CHANGE and your deliverance.

Prayer

Father, I thank You for each and every individual that is reading this book. I pray that you will help them along this journey and understand the power they have in their mouths to decree and declare over their own lives. That includes their children, their finances, and every area of their lives. May they find the strength to keep pressing despite the odds. May Your voice be the strongest in their ear and their spirit. I thank You, BIG and MIGHTY God. In Jesus' name, Amen.

Day 5

Surrounded By Love (God Surround Us With Love)

I'm grateful that when going through the many stages of challenges, I was surrounded by love. I mentioned a lot that I'm the biggest daddy's girl ever. I cannot forget mama dukes. My mom is like my best friend. I am grateful for this relationship. I can talk to her about anything, and she will not take it to anyone but God unless she thought it was something wrong and she needed to tell daddy. But she is what I call a confidant. With my many mistakes, ups, and downs, she never judged me. She loved me until I got it right. That's the amazing thing about parents; they will keep you on the altar before the Lord.

With this great example, I sought and continue to seek God to be that example for my three children, a mother who will show them the right way and a friend they can trust. A bond unbreakable. I love my mother. I have the uttermost respect for her as my mother first and then that friend I described. I also mentioned I have three brothers, two older and one younger. When I needed to go over their house and sit and express the issues of my life at that time, they always lent an ear, and they still would for their only sister. I also found that I have few friends that God has graced me with. I consider them sisters because I know they will go to war in prayer for me as I will for them. God can and will

I Am Beautifully Me:
A 7-Day Devotional of Prayer and Healing

surround you with people that will become covenant brothers and sisters to you.

In this walk, it is important to be surrounded by love. Often you can be walking and feel like you are alone. They will help pull you up and out of the low place when you go through these changes. They do not take the place of God in your life, but God allows them to be a beacon of light in your darkest situations. I went through a few years of depression and anxiety after the divorce of my childhood sweetheart. Some days I did not know if I was coming nor going. I was so lost, and I was going to church every Sunday but trying to hide what I was going through. But, when you have those covenant relationships, they can read right through a false smile. I tried my best to fake it, but I was very hurt and wanted God's help. Sisters would pick up the phone and say, "You were in my spirit, are you ok?". In those moments, I knew God heard me. I want to remind you that these people who God sends are not your savior, but they are there to help you along the journey.

If you feel you don't have those types of people in your life, pray to God that He sends those who are ordained to help carry you. You certainly need your leader, the one God sent to shepherd you. Why is this important? Because they will have a keen ear to hear the Lord concerning your life. Romans 10:14 says, "And how shall they hear without a preacher?". Where God has placed you, there you will be able to grow and receive. I am certainly grateful for great leadership.

Takeaway

The people God allows to cross your path and stay are not your savior; they assist in your journey. Love is so important because it is something that we all need. It comes in all forms. God will see to it that you are loved by Him, and then He will send love your way in the form of those meant to be a part of your life, and they will not drop you because He sent them.

Prayer

Father, I pray as You have done for myself and many others that You will surround this powerful woman of God with love. May she not search for love in all the wrong places. I pray that she will love herself with greater love and accept the love You send her way without pushing it away. I thank You in advance for the people she has and those that are on the way. You are amazing, Lord. In Jesus' name, Amen.

Day 6

Heal My Broken Spirit

The Bible says in Psalm 34:18, "The LORD is nigh unto them that are of a broken heart; and saveth such as be of a contrite spirit." He is near to those who have a broken heart. I want to share with you that when the Lord gave me the vision for *I Am Beautifully Me*, it started as a women's conference back in 2017. I was in the midst of a broken season. Not only was I physically feeling like I was not beautiful, but I was feeling broken on the inside. I had been through so much I started to feel within myself I was a failure. I felt as though there was something wrong with me.

One day as I was driving, the Lord said to me, "I Am Beautifully Me," and I carried the assignment for other women that the Lord was healing me as I was going. When He first said it, I asked, "How can I carry this assignment and this vision?" I began again to have low confidence in what God put in me. I felt like I was not qualified. I felt like how could He use me when I was in this state.

Nevertheless, I trusted His plan for my life. As I began in prayer and fasting concerning that move, God began to prune me. He began to peel back the layers of what was clouding my spirit. He began to have me look at myself in the mirror, reminding me I was created in His image. He reminded me, as I said earlier, that I was fearfully and wonderfully made. Not only was I going through not feeling good enough, but my marriage was on the rocks. Yet, I continued while God restored confidence in me.

When that conference came, I didn't even recognize myself because I was maturing, evolving, and changing for the greater. God wants to heal your broken heart. Many of you reading this book have so many great gifts in you. You have so much locked on the inside of you that God wants to pull out of you for His glory. Your story is not just for you. God gives you the victory, and you can go and encourage others in similar situations and let them know that yes, you are going through, but just as God did it for you, He can do it for them. Take in all of these moments as you watch God transform your mind, heart, and spirit. He gets you. He knows what you stand in need of. Jeremiah 1:5 says, "Before I formed thee in the belly I knew thee, and before thou camest forth out of the womb I sanctified thee." Guess what? He knew you would go through what you went through. He knew you would go down the path that you did. That goes to tell you that nothing comes as a surprise to God. Therefore, you have to learn to trust Him even more.

He comes to heal the broken spirit. He is near to you in these times. When you can't stand on your own, you stand on His word! He has great plans for you, and He wants to heal you for His glory. When He heals you, remember it is He who did it for you. He is preparing you for greater. It will not be in vain. He can take what seemed like the worst situation or season of your life, make it work for your good, and help someone else. I challenge you to look at the good in everything. We, in our human nature, automatically think negatively. But when God is the center and foundation of your life, He changes your perception. For example, relationships may fail, but you can take what you learned, how you grew, and how it helped you. Look at the good in it.

Takeaway

God comes to heal. Don't stop His process. When things happen, we want to fall apart, but that is the moment to ask God the question, "What is it that you want me to learn from this?" The reality is that some lessons we keep repeating because we stay the wheel that keeps us in a cycle. Instead, we must learn from the lesson and not do it again. Today, God heals our brokenness, and He is taking us to a place of wholeness.

I Am Beautifully Me:
A 7-Day Devotional of Prayer and Healing

Prayer

Dear God, heal every broken area of my sister's heart and spirit. Show her the lessons she is to get out of every situation so that there are NO REPEAT CYCLES. Go deep down and heal so that she may recognize her purpose on the earth. Today Lord, make it make sense to her. Open her heart that she may receive what You are trying to get to her. In Jesus' name, Amen.

Day 7

I'm Moving On

There comes a time when you have to move on. You either decide that it's time to move on, or God will send you a reminder or place you in a situation to help you realize it's time to move on. It's powerful that God cares about you enough to send His word. It may be through the written word, He may tell you through the prophet of God, or He may say it to you Himself directly. During a conference call, I shared that we should thank God when He tells us no. We always want to hear the yes from God, but no one wants to hear no. The reality is the NO saved our life. He guides us, and He knows what's best for us. Moving on is preparing you for your next.

You may be asking what am I moving on from. I want to help you today. You need to move on from downplaying who you are. For many years you felt unqualified and felt as though you didn't measure up to what God called you to do. MOVE ON. It's time to move on from wanting the acceptance of others. Not even realizing that the world's approval is something we should never seek because we are not of this world. The things of this world should not be what we desire. We are living to live again. MOVE ON. Yes, you made mistakes, and no, they were not right, but once God forgives, He forgives. Do you ever realize that you tend to let things linger and eat you up? Meanwhile, God forgave and moved on, but you haven't; it's time for you to MOVE ON.

There are many things that we all must move on from at some point in our lives. It serves us no purpose to hold onto something that the Lord calls us to let go of. I want to challenge you on this 7th day to ask the Holy Spirit how to move forward. For many of you, you have a desire to do so but don't know where to start. It all starts and ends with the Holy Spirit. He is aware of your faults as well as the good you've done. He is aware of your insecurities as well as what makes you feel confident. He is mindful of what makes you cry as well as what brings you great joy. I say this because He knows you better than you know yourself. You can certainly leave all the worries of life in His hand. He is the ONLY one able to transform your mind and spirit.

Takeaway

Today, create room for the Lord to move in your life. He desires to move in your life. According to 3 John 1:2, He wants you to prosper and be in good health. This is the will of the Father concerning you. You are a true daughter of the King. You cannot forget who you are. The room you allow Him will give Him a chance to heal you from the inside out. Moving on is not a sign of weakness, for this is when you truly learn the value of who you are.

Prayer

Father, in the name of Jesus, bless these your people. I believe that your daughters have received from this

I Am Beautifully Me:
A 7-Day Devotional of Prayer and Healing

devotional and that they will remember all that was said. I pray that they are reminded daily that You are with them. I pray that they remember daily that they are valuable. I pray that they are reminded that they are fearfully and wonderfully made. I pray that they know they are BEAUTIFUL.

I had to remember that I am beautifully me, and so are YOU!

www.ingramcontent.com/pod-product-compliance
Lightning Source LLC
Chambersburg PA
CBHW030917080526
44589CB00010B/348